MAGNIFICAT IN D
AND THE
SIX MOTETS
in Full Score

From the Bach-Gesellschaft Edition

Johann Sebastian Bach

DOVER PUBLICATIONS, INC.
New York

Bibliographical Note

This Dover edition, first published in 1995, is a new compilation of *Magnificat/D dur* and *Motetten,* originally published in Volumes 11 [1862, edited by Wilhelm Rust] and 39 [1892, edited by Franz Wüllner], respectively, of *Johann Sebastian Bach's Werke / Herausgegeben von der Bach-Gesellschaft in Leipzig* by Breitkopf & Härtel, Leipzig, n.d.
The Dover edition adds: lists of contents and instrumentation; complete texts of the works in this volume with new English translations by Stanley Appelbaum; two editorial notes; and new headings throughout.

International Standard Book Number: 0-486-28804-8

Manufactured in the United States of America
Dover Publications, Inc., 31 East 2nd Street, Mineola, N.Y. 11501

CONTENTS

*A *basso continuo* part, marked "Organo e Continuo," supports the ensemble in all sections of this work. For the *Suscepit Israel* (pp. 54–5), the supporting line is marked "Organo e Violoncelli senza Violone e Bassoni."

TEXTS AND TRANSLATIONS

English translations by Stanley Appelbaum

Magnificat

Magnificat anima mea Dominum.

Et exultavit spiritus meus in Deo salutari meo.

Quia respexit humilitatem ancillae suae; ecce enim ex hoc beatam me dicent omnes generationes.

Quia fecit mihi magna, qui potens est, et sanctum nomen ejus.

Et misericordia a progenie in progenies timentibus eum.

Fecit potentiam in brachio suo, dispersit superbos mente cordis sui.

Deposuit potentes de sede, et exaltavit humiles.

Esurientes implevit bonis, et divites dimisit inanes.

Suscepit Israel puerum suum, recordatus misericordiae suae.

Sicut locutus est ad patres nostros, Abraham et semini ejus in secula.

Gloria Patri, gloria Filio, gloria et Spiritui sancto! Sicut erat in principio, et nunc et semper et in secula seculorum, Amen.

Magnificat

My soul praises the Lord highly.

And my spirit has exulted in the God of my salvation.

For He has been mindful of the lowly status of His hand-maiden: surely, henceforth all generations will call me blessed.

For He who is mighty has done great things for me, and His name is holy.

And there is mercy from generation to generation for those who fear Him.

He has showed the strength of His arm, He has scattered the prideful by the thoughts of His heart.

He has cast down the mighty from their seats, and has lifted up the lowly.

He has filled the hungry with good things, and has sent away the rich empty-handed.

He has raised up Israel, His servant, and has remembered His mercy

(as He told our fathers) to Abraham and to his seed for all ages to come.

Glory to the Father, glory to the Son, glory also to the Holy Spirit! As it was in the beginning, so also now and for all time to come. Amen.

MOTETS

Bracketed texts are sung either antiphonally (Motet No. 1) or simultaneously (No. 4).

1. "Singet dem Herrn ein neues Lied"

Singet dem Herrn ein neues Lied, die Gemeine der Heiligen sollen ihn loben. Israel freue sich des der ihn gemacht hat. Die Kinder Zion sei'n fröhlich über ihrem Könige, sie sollen loben seinen Namen im Reigen, mit Pauken und Harfen sollen sie ihm spielen.

[CORO II] Wie sich ein Vat'r erbarmet üb'r seine junge Kinder-lein, so thut der Herr uns allen, so wir ihn kindlich fürchten rein. Er kennt das arm' Gemächte, Gott weiss, wir sind nur Staub, gleich wie das Gras vom Rechen, ein' Blum' und fallend Laub! Der Wind nur drüber wehet, so ist es nicht mehr da. Also der Mensch vergehet, sein End', das ist ihm nah'.

[CORO I] Gott, nimm dich ferner unser an, denn ohne dich ist nichts gethan mit allen unsern Sachen; Drum sei du unser Schirm und Licht, und trügt uns unsre Hoffnung nicht, so wirst du's ferner machen. Wohl dem, der sich nur steif und fest auf dich und deine Huld verlässt.

Lobet den Herrn in seinen Thaten, lobet ihn in seiner grossen Herrlichkeit! Alles, was Odem hat, lobe den Herrn, Halleluja!

1. "Sing a new song to the Lord"
[partially based on Psalm 149]

Sing a new song to the Lord, let the community of the holy praise Him. Let Israel rejoice in the One who created him. Let the children of Zion be happy in their King, let them praise His name in round dances, with drums and harps let them play to Him.

[CHORUS II] As a father takes pity on his young children, thus does the Lord with all of us as long as we fear Him with childlike purity. He knows how little strength we have, God knows we are only dust, like the grass that is raked, like flowers and falling leaves! The wind has only to blow upon them, and they no longer exist. Thus man perishes, his end is near.

[CHORUS I] God, continue to look after us, for without You none of our plans is accomplished. Thus, be our shelter and light, and, if our hope does not disappoint us, You will continue to do so. Happy the man who relies firmly and loyally on Your grace.

Praise the Lord for His deeds, praise Him for His great majesty! Let all that breathes praise the Lord, hallelujah!

2. "Der Geist hilft unsrer Schwachheit auf"

Der Geist hilft unsrer Schwachheit auf, denn wir wissen nicht, was wir beten sollen, wie sich's gebühret, sondern der Geist selbst vertritt uns auf's beste mit unaussprechlichem Seufzen. Der aber die Herzen forschet, der weiss, was des Geistes Sinn sei, denn er vertritt die Heiligen, nach dem es Gott gefället.

CHORAL: Du heilige Brunst, süsser Trost, nun hilf uns fröhlich und getrost in deinem Dienst beständig bleiben, die Trübsal uns nicht abtreiben. O Herr, durch dein' Kraft uns bereit' und stärk' des Fleisches Blödigkeit, dass wir hier ritterlich ringen, durch Tod und Leben zu dir dringen. Halleluja!

3. "Jesu, meine Freude"

CHORAL: Jesu, meine Freude, meines Herzens Weide, Jesu, meine Zier, ach, wie lange ist dem Herzen bange, und verlangt nach dir! Gottes Lamm, mein Bräutigam, ausser dir soll mir auf Erden nichts sonst Liebers werden.

Es ist nun nichts Verdammliches an denen, die in Christo Jesu sind, die nicht nach dem Fleische wandeln, sondern nach dem Geist.

CHORAL: Unter deinen Schirmen bin ich vor den Stürmen aller Feinde frei. Lass den Satan wittern, lass den Feind erbittern, mir steht Jesus bei! Ob es itzt gleich kracht und blitzt, ob gleich Sünd' und Hölle schrecken; Jesus will mich decken.

Denn das Gesetz des Geistes, der da lebendig machet in Christo Jesu, hat mich frei gemacht von dem Gesetz der Sünde und des Todes.

Trotz dem alten Drachen, Trotz des Todes Rachen, Trotz der Furcht darzu! Tobe, Welt, und springe; ich steh' hier und singe in gar sich'rer Ruh'! Gottes Macht hält mich in Acht; Erd' und Abgrund muss verstummen, ob sie noch so brummen. Ihr aber seid nicht fleischlich, sondern geistlich, so anders Gottes Geist in euch wohnet. Wer aber Christi Geist nicht hat, der ist nicht sein.

CHORAL: Weg mit allen Schätzen, du bist mein Ergötzen, Jesu, meine Lust! Weg, ihr eitlen Ehren, ich mag euch nicht hören, bleibt mir unbewusst! Elend, Noth, Kreuz, Schmach und Tod soll mich, ob ich viel muss leiden, nicht von Jesu scheiden.

So aber Christus in euch ist, so ist der Leib zwar todt um der Sünde willen; der Geist aber ist das Leben um der Gerechtigkeit willen.

Gute Nacht, o Wesen, das die Welt erlesen, mir gefällst du nicht! Gute Nacht, ihr Sünden, bleibet weit dahinten, kommt nicht mehr an's Licht! Gute Nacht, du Stolz und Pracht! Dir sei ganz, du Lasterleben, gute Nacht gegeben!

So nun der Geist dess, der Jesum von den Todten auferwecket hat, in euch wohnet; so wird auch derselbige, der Christum von den Todten auferwecket hat, eure sterblichen Leiber lebendig machen, um dess willen, dass sein Geist in euch wohnet.

CHORAL: Weicht, ihr Trauergeister, denn mein Freuden-meister, Jesus, tritt herein. Denen, die Gott lieben, muss auch ihr Betrüben lauter Zucker sein. Duld' ich schon hier Spott und Hohn, dennoch bleibst du auch im Leide, Jesu, meine Freude.

4. "Fürchte dich nicht, ich bin bei dir"

Fürchte dich nicht, ich bin bei dir, weiche nicht, denn ich, ich bin dein Gott; ich stärke dich, ich helfe dir auch, ich erhalte dich durch die rechte Hand meiner Gerechtigkeit.

⌐ Fürchte dich nicht, denn ich habe dich erlöset.
⌐ Fürchte dich nicht, ich habe dich bei deinem Namen gerufen.

2. "The Spirit helps us in our weakness"

The Spirit helps us in our weakness, for we do not know what to pray for, or what is proper; but the Spirit itself intercedes for us best of all with inexpressible sighing. But He who examines our hearts knows what our mind intends, for He is the spokesman of the holy, as it pleases God.

CHORALE: You holy ardor, sweet comfort, now help us to remain perpetually in Your service with joy and solace, let affliction not drive us away. O Lord, prepare us through Your might and strengthen the weakness of our flesh, so that we can struggle here like knights and attain to You through death and life. Hallelujah!

3. "Jesus, my joy"

CHORALE: Jesus, my joy, pleasure of my heart; Jesus, my adornment, oh, how long my heart has been afraid and yearning for You! Lamb of God, my bridegroom, there shall be nothing on earth more dear to me than You.

Now, there is nothing to condemn in those who are in Jesus Christ, who do not walk in the way of the flesh but follow the spirit.

CHORALE: Under your protection I am safe from the raging of every enemy. Let Satan storm, let the enemy grow cruel, Jesus is at my side! Even though it now thunders and lightens, even though sin and hell frighten me, Jesus will be my shield.

For the law of the Spirit that gives us life in Jesus Christ has made me free from the law of sin and death.

Defiance to the old dragon, defiance to the jaws of death, defiance to the fear of it! Rage and leap, O world; I remain here singing in the most perfect repose! God's might is watching over me; the earth and the abyss must fall silent, no matter how they rumble. But you are not fleshly, but spiritual, when God's spirit dwells in you. But the man who does not possess Christ's spirit is not His.

CHORALE: Away with all treasures, You are my delight, Jesus, my pleasure! Away, you vain honors, I do not want to hear you, remain unknown to me! Misery, distress, the cross, shame and death—even though I must suffer greatly—shall not separate me from Jesus.

But if Jesus is in you, your body is dead with regard to sin, but the spirit is life for the sake of justice.

Farewell to the conduct that the world has chosen—I do not like you! Farewell to sin—stay far from me, do not appear in the light anymore! Farewell to pride and pomp! And farewell forever to a life of vice!

As long as the spirit of the One who raised up Jesus from the dead dwells in you, the same One who raised up Christ from the dead will give life to your mortal bodies, so that His spirit may dwell in you.

CHORALE: Vanish, spirits of sadness, for the master of my joy, Jesus, is entering. For those who love God, even their sorrow must be all sweetness. If here I undergo mockery and scorn, nevertheless even in grief, Jesus, you remain my joy.

4. "Do not fear, I am with you"

Do not fear, I am with you, do not flee, for I am your God; I will strengthen you, I will also help you, I will sustain you with the right hand of My justice.

⌐ Do not fear, for I have redeemed you.
⌐ Do not fear, I have called you by your name.

Herr, mein Hirt, Brunn aller Freuden! Du bist mein, ich bin dein; niemand kann uns scheiden: Ich bin dein, weil du dein Leben und dein Blut, mir zu gut, in den Tod gegeben. Du bist mein, weil ich dich fasse, und dich nicht, o mein Licht! aus dem Herzen lasse! Lass mich hin gelangen, wo du mich, und ich dich ewig werd' umfangen.

Fürchte dich nicht, du bist mein.

5. "Komm, Jesu, komm"

Komm, Jesu, komm, mein Leib ist müde, die Kraft verschwind't je mehr und mehr, ich sehne mich nach deinem Friede; der saure Weg wird mir zu schwer! Komm, ich will mich dir ergeben, du bist der rechte Weg, die Wahrheit und das Leben.

"ARIA": Drauf schliess' ich mich in deine Hände und sage, Welt, zu guter Nacht! eilt gleich mein Lebenslauf zu Ende, ist doch der Geist wohl angebracht. Er soll bei seinem Schöpfer schweben, weil Jesus ist und bleibt der wahre Weg zum Leben.

6. "Lobet den Herrn, alle Heiden"

Lobet den Herrn, alle Heiden, und preiset ihn, alle Völker. Denn seine Gnade und Wahrheit waltet über uns in Ewigkeit. Alleluja.

Lord, my shepherd, fountain of all joys! You are mine, I am Yours; no one can part us: I am Yours because You gave over to death Your life and Your blood, too precious for me. You are mine because I grasp You and—O my light!—will not let You out of my heart! Let me reach the place where You will eternally embrace me, and I You.

Do not fear, you are Mine.

5. "Come, Jesus, come"

Come, Jesus, come, my body is weary, my strength is ebbing more and more all the time, I long for Your peace; the bitter path is becoming too hard for me! Come, I will surrender myself to You, You are the right path, truth and life.

"ARIA": Then I enclose myself within Your hands and bid the world farewell! Even if my span of life is hastening to its end, my spirit has found a good lodging. It will soar beside its Creator, because Jesus is and remains the true path to life.

6. "Praise the Lord, all heathen nations"
[based on Psalm 117]

Praise the Lord, all heathen nations, and laud Him, all peoples. For His mercy and truth reign over us eternally. Hallelujah.

MAGNIFICAT IN D

BWV 243, *ca.* 1728–31

For solo vocal quintet (SSATB),
chorus (SSATB) and orchestra

NOTE

On the great feast days, the Magnificat was given at the evening service in Leipzig, following the sermon. Bach twice set this poem (Luke I, 46–55). One of these compositions, for solo soprano, has been lost. Of the other Magnificat, Bach composed his first version, in E-flat, with four inserted Christmas pieces, prepared for the evening service of that holiday, 1723. His revision of 1728–31, in D major, omitting the Christmas movements, was intended for use on any major feast day.

INSTRUMENTATION

3 Trumpets in D [Tromba]

Timpani [Timpani]

2 Flutes [Flauto traverso]

2 Oboes [Oboe]
    doubling[?]
2 Oboes d'amore [Oboe d'amore]

Violins I, II [Violino]

Violas [Viola]

    Solo Vocal Quintet [SSATB]

    Chorus [SSATB]

Continuo: Organ [Organo] with optional low strings and woodwinds of the period. The score (see *Suscepit Israel,* p. 54) specifies only *Violoncelli* (cellos), *Violone* (string bass) and *Bassoni* (bassoons).

sit
on
cue

fe _ cit po _ ten _ tiam,   fe _ cit po _ ten _ tiam,

_ ti _ am in bra _ _ chi _ o su _ o,   po _ ten _ tiam,   fe _ cit po _ ten _ tiam   in bra _ _ chi _ o su _

o, di _ sper _ _ _ _ _ _ sit, fecit po _ ten _ tiam,   fe _ cit po _ ten _ tiam, di _ sper _ _ _ _ sit, dispersit,

di _ sper _ _ _ _ _ sit, fecit po _ ten _ tiam,   fe _ cit po _ ten _ tiam, di _ sper _ sit,   dispersit,   di _

fe _ cit   po _ ten _ _ _ _ _ _ _ _ _ _ _ _ _ _

12

Adagio.

Flauto traverso I.

Flauto traverso II.

Alto.

Organo e
Continuo.

pizzicato

E _ su _ ri _ en _ tes im _ ple _ _ _ vit bo _ nis, e _ su _ ri _ en _ tes im _ ple _ _ vit bo _ nis, et

di _ vi _ tes di _ mi _ sit, et di _ vi _ tes di _ mi _ sit, di _ mi _ sit in _ a _ nes, et

AW

SIX MOTETS

NOTE

Bach composed the motets for special occasions, probably for the birthdays, funerals or memorial services of prominent Leipzig citizens.[1]

In this edition, five of the six motets are scored for *a cappella* chorus: Nos. 1, 2, 4 and 5 for double chorus (SATB/SATB), No. 3 for various combinations of three-, four- and five-part voices. Motet No. 6 is scored for SATB and continuo.

According to *Grove*,[2] "It was a rule in the performance of motets at Leipzig . . . that a continuo part should be included—to be precise, a harpsichord and string bass. The performing parts that have survived for *Der Geist hilft* [Motet No. 2], with strings (first chorus) and reed instruments [two oboes da caccia and bassoon] (second chorus) doubling the voices, cannot necessarily be taken as applicable to the other motets."

Philipp Spitta adds: "[According to Bach's student Johann Kirnberger], 'Performances of church-music, even when sung . . . without instruments, were always accompanied on the organ . . . Another arrangement was to accompany each voice part with trumpets and cornets, but never without due reference to the employment of at least one organ manual.'"

---

[1]For the most part, the occasions for which the motets were written are conjectural. This and related topics, including likely dates of composition, are discussed in the following Dover publications:

- Albert Schweitzer, *J. S. Bach* (English translation by Ernest Newman). Vol. 2 of two volumes: Chap. XXXI, pp. 294–300. Dover, 1966 (0-486-21632-2).
- Philipp Spitta, *Johann Sebastian Bach* (Unabridged Edition). Vol. 2 of three volumes: pp. 594–612. Dover, 1992 (0-486-27413-6).
- Charles Sanford Terry, *The Music of Bach: An Introduction*. Chap. VIII, pp. 84–7. Dover, 1963 (0-486-21075-8).

[2]*The New Grove Dictionary of Music and Musicians*, Vol. 1, pp. 810–11. Macmillian Publishers Limited, London, 1980.

1. "Singet dem Herrn ein neues Lied"

["Sing a new song to the Lord"]

BWV 225, 1727[?]

Motets: 1. "Singet dem Herrn ein neues Lied"

Motets: 1. "Singet dem Herrn ein neues Lied"

Motets: 1. "Singet dem Herrn ein neues Lied"

Motets: 1. "Singet dem Herrn ein neues Lied"

Motets: 1. "Singet dem Herrn ein neues Lied"

Motets: 1. "Singet dem Herrn ein neues Lied"

Motets: 1. "Singet dem Herrn ein neues Lied"

Motets: 1. "Singet dem Herrn ein neues Lied"

Motets: 1. "Singet dem Herrn ein neues Lied"

Motets: 1. "Singet dem Herrn ein neues Lied"

Motets: 1. "Singet dem Herrn ein neues Lied"

Motets: 1. "Singet dem Herrn ein neues Lied"

2. "Der Geist hilft unsrer Schwachheit auf"

["The Spirit helps us in our weakness"]

BWV 226, 1729

Motets: 2. "Der Geist hilft unsrer Schwachheit auf"

Motets: 2. "Der Geist hilft unsrer Schwachheit auf"

Motets: 2. "Der Geist hilft unsrer Schwachheit auf"

Motets: 2. "Der Geist hilft unsrer Schwachheit auf"

3. "Jesu, meine Freude"

["Jesus, my joy"]

BWV 227, 1723[?]

CHORAL.

Soprano.

Je_su, mei_ne Freu _ de, mei_nes Her_zens Wei _ de, Je_su, mei_ne Zier,

Alto.

Je_su, meine Freu _ de, meines Her_zens Wei _ de, Je_su, mei_ne Zier,

Tenore.

Je_su, mei_ne Freu _ de, mei_nes Her_zens Wei _ de, Je_su, mei_ne Zier,

Basso.

Je_su, mei _ ne Freu _ de, mei_nes Her_zens Wei _ de, Je_su, mei_ne Zier,

ach, wie lang', ach, lan _ ge ist dem Her_zen ban _ ge, und ver_langt nach dir!

ach, wie lang',ach, lan _ ge ist dem Her_zen ban _ ge, und ver_langt nach dir!

ach, wie lang',ach, lan _ ge ist dem Her_zen ban _ ge, und ver_langt nach dir!

ach, wie lang', ach, lan _ ge ist dem Her_zen ban _ ge, und ver_langt nach dir!

Gottes Lamm,mein Bräu _ tigam, au_sser dir soll mir auf Er _ den nichts sonst Lie_bers wer_ _ den.

Gottes Lamm,mein Bräuti _ gam, au_sser dir soll mir auf Er _ den nichts sonst Lie_bers wer_ _ den.

Gottes Lamm,mein Bräu_ti_gam, au_sser dir soll mir auf Er _ den nichts sonst Liebers wer_ _ den.

GottesLamm,mein Bräuti _ gam, au_sser dir soll mir auf Er_ _ den nichts sonst Lie_bers wer_ _ den.

Motets: 3. "Jesu, meine Freude"

CHORAL.

Soprano. Weg mit al _ len Schä _ tzen, du bist mein Er _

Alto. Weg, weg mit al _ len Schä _ tzen, mit al_len Schätzen, du, du bist

Tenore. Weg, weg, weg, weg mit al_len Schä _ tzen, mit al_len Schä_tzen, du, du bist

Basso. Weg, weg, weg, weg mit al_len Schätzen, du, du bist mein Er _ gö _

gö _ tzen, Je _ su, mei _ ne Lust! Weg, ihr eit _ len

mein Er _ gö _ tzen, Je _ su, mei _ ne Lust, mei _ ne Lust! Weg, weg, ihr eit _ len

mein Er _ gö _ tzen, Je _ su, mei _ _ ne Lust! Weg, weg, weg, weg, ihr eit _ len

_ _ tzen, Je _ su, Je _ su, mei _ ne Lust, mei _ ne Lust! Weg, weg, weg, weg, ihr

CHORAL.

Soprano. Weicht, ihr Trau_er_gei_ster, denn mein Freuden_mei_ster, Je_sus, tritt her_ein.

Alto. Weicht, ihr Trau_er_gei_ster, denn mein Freuden_mei_ster, Je_sus, tritt her_ein.

Tenore. Weicht, ihr Trau_er_gei_ster, denn mein Freu_den_mei_ster, Je_sus, tritt her_ein.

Basso. Weicht, ihr Trau_er_gei_ster, denn mein Freu_den_mei_ster, Je_sus, tritt her_ein.

De_nen, die Gott lie_ben, muss auch ihr Be_trü_ben lau_ter Zu_cker sein.

De_nen, die Gott lie_ben, muss auch ihr Be_trü_ben lau_ter Zu_cker sein.

De_nen, die Gott lie_ben, muss auch ihr Be_trü_ben lau_ter Zu_cker sein.

De_nen, die Gott lie_ben, muss auch ihr Be_trü_ben lau_ter Zu_cker sein.

Duld' ich schon hier Spott und Hohn, dennoch bleibst du auch im Lei_de, Je_su, mei_ne Freu_de.

Duld' ich schon hier Spott und Hohn, dennoch bleibst du auch im Lei_de, Je_su, mei_ne Freu_de.

Duld' ich schon hier Spott und Hohn, dennoch bleibst du auch im Lei_de, Je_su, mei_ne Freu_de.

Duld' ich schon hier Spott und Hohn, den_noch bleibst du auch im Lei_de, Je_su, mei_ne Freu_de.

4. "Fürchte dich nicht, ich bin bei dir"

["Do not fear, I am with you"]

BWV 228, 1726[?]

Motets: 4. "Fürchte dich nicht, ich bin bei dir"

Motets: 4. "Fürchte dich nicht, ich bin bei dir"

Motets: 4. "Fürchte dich nicht, ich bin bei dir"

Motets: 4. ''Fürchte dich nicht, ich bin bei dir''

5. "Komm, Jesu, komm"

["Come, Jesus, come"]

BWV 229, 1730

165

6. "Lobet den Herrn, alle Heiden"

["Praise the Lord, all heathen nations"]

BWV 118, uncertain date

END OF EDITION

Motets: 6. "Lobet den Herrn, alle Heiden"

Dover Orchestral Scores

THE SIX BRANDENBURG CONCERTOS AND THE FOUR ORCHESTRAL SUITES IN FULL SCORE, Johann Sebastian Bach. Complete standard Bach-Gesellschaft editions in large, clear format. Study score. 273pp. 9 × 12.   23376-6 Pa. **$10.95**

COMPLETE CONCERTI FOR SOLO KEYBOARD AND ORCHESTRA IN FULL SCORE, Johann Sebastian Bach. Bach's seven complete concerti for solo keyboard and orchestra in full score from the authoritative Bach-Gesellschaft edition. 206pp. 9 × 12.   24929-8 Pa. **$10.95**

THE THREE VIOLIN CONCERTI IN FULL SCORE, Johann Sebastian Bach. Concerto in A Minor, BWV 1041; Concerto in E Major, BWV 1042; and Concerto for Two Violins in D Minor, BWV 1043. Bach-Gesellschaft edition. 64pp. 9⅜ × 12¼.   25124-1 Pa. **$5.95**

GREAT ORGAN CONCERTI, OPP. 4 & 7, IN FULL SCORE, George Frideric Handel. 12 organ concerti composed by great Baroque master are reproduced in full score from the *Deutsche Handelgesellschaft* edition. 138pp. 9⅜ × 12¼.   24462-8 Pa. **$8.95**

COMPLETE CONCERTI GROSSI IN FULL SCORE, George Frideric Handel. Monumental Opus 6 Concerti Grossi, Opus 3 and "Alexander's Feast" Concerti Grossi—19 in all—reproduced from most authoritative edition. 258pp. 9⅜ × 12¼.   24187-4 Pa. **$12.95**

COMPLETE CONCERTI GROSSI IN FULL SCORE, Arcangelo Corelli. All 12 concerti in the famous late nineteenth-century edition prepared by violinist Joseph Joachim and musicologist Friedrich Chrysander. 240pp. 8⅜ × 11¼.   25606-5 Pa. **$12.95**

WATER MUSIC AND MUSIC FOR THE ROYAL FIREWORKS IN FULL SCORE, George Frideric Handel. Full scores of two of the most popular Baroque orchestral works performed today—reprinted from definitive Deutsche Handelgesellschaft edition. Total of 96pp. 8⅜ × 11.   25070-9 Pa. **$6.95**

LATER SYMPHONIES, Wolfgang A. Mozart. Full orchestral scores to last symphonies (Nos. 35–41) reproduced from definitive Breitkopf & Härtel Complete Works edition. Study score. 285pp. 9 × 12.   23052-X Pa. **$11.95**

17 DIVERTIMENTI FOR VARIOUS INSTRUMENTS, Wolfgang A. Mozart. Sparkling pieces of great vitality and brilliance from 1771–1779; consecutively numbered from 1 to 17. Reproduced from definitive Breitkopf & Härtel Complete Works edition. Study score. 241pp. 9⅜ × 12¼.   23862-8 Pa. **$11.95**

PIANO CONCERTOS NOS. 11–16 IN FULL SCORE, Wolfgang Amadeus Mozart. Authoritative Breitkopf & Härtel edition of six staples of the concerto repertoire, including Mozart's cadenzas for Nos. 12–16. 256pp. 9⅜ × 12¼.   25468-2 Pa. **$12.95**

PIANO CONCERTOS NOS. 17–22, Wolfgang Amadeus Mozart. Six complete piano concertos in full score, with Mozart's own cadenzas for Nos. 17–19. Breitkopf & Härtel edition. Study score. 370pp. 9⅜ × 12¼.   23599-8 Pa. **$14.95**

PIANO CONCERTOS NOS. 23–27, Wolfgang Amadeus Mozart. Mozart's last five piano concertos in full score, plus cadenzas for Nos. 23 and 27, and the Concert Rondo in D Major, K.382. Breitkopf & Härtel edition. Study score. 310pp. 9⅜ × 12¼.   23600-5 Pa. **$12.95**

CONCERTI FOR WIND INSTRUMENTS IN FULL SCORE, Wolfgang Amadeus Mozart. Exceptional volume contains ten pieces for orchestra and wind instruments and includes some of Mozart's finest, most popular music. 272pp. 9⅜ × 12¼.   25228-0 Pa. **$12.95**

THE VIOLIN CONCERTI AND THE SINFONIA CONCERTANTE, K.364, IN FULL SCORE, Wolfgang Amadeus Mozart. All five violin concerti and famed double concerto reproduced from authoritative Breitkopf & Härtel Complete Works Edition. 208pp. 9⅜ × 12½.   25169-1 Pa. **$11.95**

SYMPHONIES 88–92 IN FULL SCORE: The Haydn Society Edition, Joseph Haydn. Full score of symphonies Nos. 88 through 92. Large, readable noteheads, ample margins for fingerings, etc., and extensive Editor's Commentary. 304pp. 9 × 12. (Available in U.S. only)   24445-8 Pa. **$13.95**

COMPLETE LONDON SYMPHONIES IN FULL SCORE, Series I and Series II, Joseph Haydn. Reproduced from the Eulenburg editions are Symphonies Nos. 93–98 (Series I) and Nos. 99–104 (Series II). 800pp. 8⅜ × 11¼. (Available in U.S. only)   Series I 24982-4 Pa. **$15.95**   Series II 24983-2 Pa. **$16.95**

FOUR SYMPHONIES IN FULL SCORE, Franz Schubert. Schubert's four most popular symphonies: No. 4 in C Minor ("Tragic"); No. 5 in B-flat Major; No. 8 in B Minor ("Unfinished"); and No. 9 in C Major ("Great"). Breitkopf & Härtel edition. Study score. 261pp. 9⅜ × 12¼.   23681-1 Pa. **$11.95**

GREAT OVERTURES IN FULL SCORE, Carl Maria von Weber. Overtures to *Oberon, Der Freischutz, Euryanthe* and *Preciosa* reprinted from auhoritative Breitkopf & Härtel editions. 112pp. 9 × 12.   25225-6 Pa. **$8.95**

SYMPHONIES NOS. 1, 2, 3, AND 4 IN FULL SCORE, Ludwig van Beethoven. Republication of H. Litolff edition. 272pp. 9 × 12.   26033-X Pa. **$10.95**

SYMPHONIES NOS. 5, 6 AND 7 IN FULL SCORE, Ludwig van Beethoven. Republication of the H. Litolff edition. 272pp. 9 × 12.   26034-8 Pa. **$10.95**

SYMPHONIES NOS. 8 AND 9 IN FULL SCORE, Ludwig van Beethoven. Republication of the H. Litolff edition. 256pp. 9 × 12.   26035-6 Pa. **$10.95**

SIX GREAT OVERTURES IN FULL SCORE, Ludwig van Beethoven. Six staples of the orchestral repertoire from authoritative Breitkopf & Härtel edition. *Leonore Overtures*, Nos. 1–3; Overtures to *Coriolanus, Egmont, Fidelio.* 288pp. 9 × 12.   24789-9 Pa. **$12.95**

COMPLETE PIANO CONCERTOS IN FULL SCORE, Ludwig van Beethoven. Complete scores of five great Beethoven piano concertos, with all cadenzas as he wrote them, reproduced from authoritative Breitkopf & Härtel edition. New table of contents. 384pp. 9⅜ × 12¼.   24563-2 Pa. **$14.95**

GREAT ROMANTIC VIOLIN CONCERTI IN FULL SCORE, Ludwig van Beethoven, Felix Mendelssohn and Peter Ilyitch Tchaikovsky. The Beethoven Op. 61, Mendelssohn, Op. 64 and Tchaikovsky, Op. 35 concertos reprinted from the Breitkopf & Härtel editions. 224pp. 9 × 12.   24989-1 Pa. **$10.95**

MAJOR ORCHESTRAL WORKS IN FULL SCORE, Felix Mendelssohn. Generally considered to be Mendelssohn's finest orchestral works, here in one volume are: the complete *Midsummer Night's Dream; Hebrides Overture; Calm Sea and Prosperous Voyage Overture;* Symphony No. 3 in A ("Scottish"); and Symphony No. 4 in A ("Italian"). Breitkopf & Härtel edition. Study score. 406pp. 9 × 12.   23184-4 Pa. **$16.95**

COMPLETE SYMPHONIES, Johannes Brahms. Full orchestral scores. No. 1 in C Minor, Op. 68; No. 2 in D Major, Op. 73; No. 3 in F Major, Op. 90; and No. 4 in E Minor, Op. 98. Reproduced from definitive Vienna Gesellschaft der Musikfreunde edition. Study score. 344pp. 9 × 12.   23053-8 Pa. **$13.95**

*Available from your music dealer or write for **free** Music Catalog to*
Dover Publications, Inc., Dept. MUBI, 31 East 2nd Street, Mineola, N.Y. 11501.

Dover Chamber Music Scores

COMPLETE SUITES FOR UNACCOMPANIED CELLO AND SONATAS FOR VIOLA DA GAMBA, Johann Sebastian Bach. Bach-Gesellschaft edition of the six cello suites (BWV 1007–1012) and three sonatas (BWV 1027–1029), commonly played today on the cello. 112pp. 9⅜ × 12¼. 25641-3 Pa. **$8.95**

WORKS FOR VIOLIN, Johann Sebastian Bach. Complete Sonatas and Partitas for Unaccompanied Violin; Six Sonatas for Violin and Clavier. Bach-Gesellschaft edition. 158pp. 9⅜ × 12¼. 23683-8 Pa. **$8.95**

COMPLETE STRING QUARTETS, Wolfgang A. Mozart. Breitkopf & Härtel edition. All 23 string quartets plus alternate slow movement to K.156. Study score. 277pp. 9⅜ × 12¼. 22372-8 Pa. **$12.95**

COMPLETE STRING QUINTETS, Wolfgang Amadeus Mozart. All the standard-instrumentation string quintets, plus String Quintet in C Minor, K.406; Quintet with Horn or Second Cello, K.407; and Clarinet Quintet, K.581. Breitkopf & Härtel edition. Study score. 181pp. 9⅜ × 12¼. 23603-X Pa. **$8.95**

STRING QUARTETS, OPP. 20 and 33, COMPLETE, Joseph Haydn. Complete reproductions of the 12 masterful quartets (six each) of Opp. 20 and 33—in the reliable Eulenburg edition. 272pp. 8⅜ × 11¼. 24852-6 Pa. **$12.95**

STRING QUARTETS, OPP. 42, 50 and 54, Joseph Haydn. Complete reproductions of Op. 42 in D minor; Op. 50, Nos. 1–6 ("Prussian Quartets") and Op. 54, Nos. 1–3. Reliable Eulenburg edition. 224pp. 8⅜ × 11¼. 24262-5 Pa. **$11.95**

TWELVE STRING QUARTETS, Joseph Haydn. 12 often-performed works: Op. 55, Nos. 1–3 (including *Razor*); Op. 64, Nos. 1–6; Op. 71, Nos. 1–3. Definitive Eulenburg edition. 288pp. 8⅜ × 11¼. 23933-0 Pa. **$11.95**

ELEVEN LATE STRING QUARTETS, Joseph Haydn. Complete reproductions of Op. 74, Nos. 1–3; Op. 76, Nos. 1–6; and Op. 77, Nos. 1 and 2. Definitive Eulenburg edition. Full-size study score. 320pp. 8⅜ × 11¼. 23753-2 Pa. **$12.95**

COMPLETE STRING QUARTETS, Ludwig van Beethoven. Breitkopf & Härtel edition. Six quartets of Opus 18; three quartets of Opus 59; Opera 74, 95, 127, 130, 131, 132, 135 and Grosse Fuge. Study score. 434pp. 9⅜ × 12¼. 22361-2 Pa. **$15.95**

SIX GREAT PIANO TRIOS IN FULL SCORE, Ludwig van Beethoven. Definitive Breitkopf & Härtel edition of Beethoven's Piano Trios Nos. 1–6 including the "Ghost" and the "Archduke". 224pp. 9⅜ × 12¼. 25398-8 Pa. **$10.95**

COMPLETE VIOLIN SONATAS, Ludwig van Beethoven. All ten sonatas including the "Kreutzer" and "Spring" sonatas in the definitive Breitkopf & Härtel edition. 256pp. 9 × 12. 26277-4 Pa. **$12.95**

COMPLETE SONATAS AND VARIATIONS FOR CELLO AND PIANO, Ludwig van Beethoven. All five sonatas and three sets of variations. Reprinted from Breitkopf & Härtel edition. 176pp. 9⅜ × 12¼. 26441-6 Pa. **$10.95**

COMPLETE CHAMBER MUSIC FOR STRINGS, Franz Schubert. Reproduced from famous Breitkopf & Härtel edition: Quintet in C Major (1828), 15 quartets and two trios for violin(s), viola, and violincello. Study score. 348pp. 9 × 12. 21463-X Pa. **$14.95**

COMPLETE CHAMBER MUSIC FOR PIANOFORTE AND STRINGS, Franz Schubert. Breitkopf & Härtel edition. *Trout,* Quartet in F Major, and trios for piano, violin, cello. Study score. 192pp. 9 × 12. 21527-X Pa. **$9.95**

CHAMBER WORKS FOR PIANO AND STRINGS, Felix Mendelssohn. Eleven of the composer's best known works in the genre—duos, trios, quartets and a sextet—reprinted from authoritative Breitkopf & Härtel edition. 384pp. 9⅜ × 12¼. 26117-4 Pa. **$15.95**

COMPLETE CHAMBER MUSIC FOR STRINGS, Felix Mendelssohn. All of Mendelssohn's chamber music: Octet, Two Quintets, Six Quartets, and Four Pieces for String Quartet. (Nothing with piano is included). Complete works edition (1874–7). Study score. 283pp. 9⅜ × 12¼. 23679-X Pa. **$12.95**

CHAMBER MUSIC OF ROBERT SCHUMANN, edited by Clara Schumann. Superb collection of three trios, four quartets, and piano quintet. Breitkopf & Härtel edition. 288pp. 9⅜ × 12¼. 24101-7 Pa. **$12.95**

COMPLETE SONATAS FOR SOLO INSTRUMENT AND PIANO, Johannes Brahms. All seven sonatas—three for violin, two for cello and two for clarinet (or viola)—reprinted from the authoritative Breitkopf & Härtel edition. 208pp. 9 × 12. 26091-7 Pa. **$11.95**

COMPLETE CHAMBER MUSIC FOR STRINGS AND CLARINET QUINTET, Johannes Brahms. Vienna Gesellschaft der Musikfreunde edition of all quartets, quintets, and sextet without piano. Study edition. 262pp. 8⅜ × 11¼. 21914-3 Pa. **$11.95**

QUINTET AND QUARTETS FOR PIANO AND STRINGS, Johannes Brahms. Full scores of *Quintet in F Minor,* Op. 34; *Quartet in G Minor,* Op. 25; *Quartet in A Major,* Op. 26; *Quartet in C Minor,* Op. 60. Breitkopf & Härtel edition. 298pp. 9 × 12. 24900-X Pa. **$13.95**

COMPLETE PIANO TRIOS, Johannes Brahms. All five piano trios in the definitive Breitkopf & Härtel edition. 288pp. 9 × 12. 25769-X Pa. **$13.95**

CHAMBER WORKS FOR PIANO AND STRINGS, Antonín Dvorák. Society editions of the F Minor and Dumky piano trios, D Major and E-flat Major piano quartets and A Major piano quintet. 352pp. 8⅜ × 11¼. (Available in U.S. only) 25663-4 Pa. **$15.95**

FIVE LATE STRING QUARTETS, Antonín Dvorák. Treasury of Czech master's finest chamber works: Nos. 10, 11, 12, 13, 14. Reliable Simrock editions. 282pp. 8⅛ × 11. 25135-7 Pa. **$11.95**

STRING QUARTETS BY DEBUSSY AND RAVEL/Claude Debussy: Quartet in G Minor, Op. 10/Maurice Ravel: Quartet in F Major, Claude Debussy and Maurice Ravel. Authoritative one-volume edition of two influential masterpieces noted for individuality, delicate and subtle beauties. 112pp. 8⅛ × 11. (Not available in France or Germany) 25231-0 Pa. **$7.95**

GREAT CHAMBER WORKS, César Franck. Four Great works: Violin Sonata in A Major, Piano Trio in F-sharp Minor, String Quartet in D Major and Piano Quintet in F Minor. From J. Hamelle, Paris and C. F. Peters, Leipzig editions. 248pp. 9⅜ × 12¼. **26546-3 Pa. $13.95**

Available from your music dealer or write for ***free*** *Music Catalog to*
Dover Publications, Inc., Dept. MUBI, 31 East 2nd Street, Mineola, N.Y. 11501.